Dearest Lucy,

For your first Christmas, your Aunt and I wanted to give you the gift of reading a book. May God bless you now and always.

Love,
Uncle Jon & Aunt Linda

My Twelve
MAINE
CHRISTMAS
DAYS

My Twelve
MAINE
CHRISTMAS
DAYS

by **Wendy Ulmer**
artwork by **Sandy Crabtree**

Enjoy the gifts of Maine!

wendy k ulmer

wooly moon books  Maine • USA

wooly moon books
PO Box 274
Woolwich, ME 04579

www.wendyulmer.com
woolymoon@gmail.com

Printed and bound in the United States of America
First Edition
Fourth Printing, 2016
LCCN 2014943547
ISBN 978-0-692-23991-9

This book was expertly produced by Book Bridge Press.
www.bookbridgepress.com

For Tucker, who loves lobster,
and for Gene and Nancy,
who keep Maine close
in their hearts

—W. U.

To Colin, Gage,
and Greta, my
grandchildren,
whose joy in
everyday things
inspires thousands
of pictures

—S. C.

On my first Maine Christmas
a woodsman gave to me

one dark-green wild pine tree.

On my second Maine Christmas
a boat builder gave to me

2

two wooden oars

and a dark-green wild pine tree.

On my third Maine Christmas
a lobsterman gave to me

3 three blue lobsters,

two wooden oars,
and a dark-green wild pine tree.

On my fourth Maine Christmas
a farmer gave to me

4 four new potatoes,

three blue lobsters,
two wooden oars,
and a dark-green wild pine tree.

On my fifth Maine Christmas
a ranger gave to me

five majestic moose,

four new potatoes,
three blue lobsters,
two wooden oars,
and a dark-green wild pine tree.

On my sixth Maine Christmas
a knitter gave to me

6 **six woolen mittens,**

five majestic moose,
four new potatoes,
three blue lobsters,
two wooden oars,
and a dark-green wild pine tree.

On my seventh Maine Christmas
a beachcomber gave to me

7 seven sand dollars,

six woolen mittens,
five majestic moose,
four new potatoes,
three blue lobsters,
two wooden oars,
and a dark-green wild pine tree.

On my eighth Maine Christmas
a shrimper gave to me

8 **eight shiny shrimp,**

seven sand dollars,
six woolen mittens,
five majestic moose,
four new potatoes,
three blue lobsters,
two wooden oars,
and a dark-green wild pine tree.

On my ninth Maine Christmas
a baker gave to me

9 nine whoopie pies,

eight shiny shrimp,
seven sand dollars,
six woolen mittens,
five majestic moose,
four new potatoes,
three blue lobsters,
two wooden oars,
and a dark-green wild pine tree.

On my tenth Maine Christmas
a digger gave to me

10

ten spitting clams,

nine whoopie pies,
eight shiny shrimp,
seven sand dollars,
six woolen mittens,
five majestic moose,
four new potatoes,
three blue lobsters,
two wooden oars,
and a dark-green wild pine tree.

On my eleventh Maine Christmas
a picker gave to me

eleven blueberries,

ten spitting clams,
nine whoopie pies,
eight shiny shrimp,
seven sand dollars,
six woolen mittens,
five majestic moose,
four new potatoes,
three blue lobsters,
two wooden oars,
and a dark-green wild pine tree.

On my twelfth Maine Christmas
a birder gave to me

12 twelve chickadees,

eleven blueberries, ten spitting clams,
nine whoopie pies, eight shiny shrimp,
seven sand dollars, six woolen mittens,
five majestic moose, four new potatoes,
three blue lobsters, two wooden oars,
and a dark-green wild pine tree.

Learn more about Maine,
and discover the places that inspired each painting

Pine Tree

Maine is nicknamed the Pine Tree State. Maine named the Eastern White Pine the state tree in 1945, and the state flower is the white pine cone and tassel. The Eastern White Pine is the tallest tree in eastern North America. In the 1700s, the tallest, straightest pines were marked with the King's Broad Arrow and used for the masts of sailing ships. They were known as the "King's pines." Close to 90 percent of Maine is forested. (Moosehead Region)

Wooden Oars

Shipbuilding in Maine began in 1607 near Bath, where shipbuilding is still prominent today. Oars from Maine are made in sizes for children and up to more than 20 feet long for larger boats. Shaw and Tenney from Orono is the second oldest manufacturer of marine products in the United States. (Monhegan Island)

Blue Lobsters

Maine established the first commercial lobster fishery in the 1840s. Lobstering is done all year, but the majority of lobsters are caught from late June to late December. A rare genetic variation causes some lobsters to turn blue. (Fort Popham, Phippsburg)

Potatoes

Maine is eighth in the nation in the production of fall potatoes, and the potato is the main agricultural product of northern Maine. Ninety percent of Maine potatoes are grown in Aroostook County. Two varieties of Maine potatoes are the Kennebec and the Katahdin. (Aroostook County)

Moose

The moose was named the official state animal in 1979. It is the largest member of the deer family. Maine has one of the largest moose populations in the country. The Algonquian Native Americans called them mooswa, which means "animal that strips bark from trees." (Moosehead Region)

Mittens

Knitted mitten patterns are often handed down from mothers to daughters. Maine mitten tips are rounded. The original fishermen mittens were made quite large, soaked in icy salt water, and then placed on the engine to dry and shrink. Men in the lumber camps double-knit their mittens and covered them with horsehide. (Bath)

Sand Dollars

A sand dollar is the skeleton of a marine animal. Sand dollars have five sets of pores in a petal pattern used to push water in and out to help them move. They live just beyond the low water mark beneath the sand surface. People often collect them as keepsakes and for jewelry. (Sand Dollar Beach, Hermit Island, Phippsburg)

Shrimp

Wild Maine shrimp live on the muddy sea floor in the Gulf of Maine. Some years Maine fishermen catch more than 90 percent of the Northeast harvest. (Five Islands, Georgetown)

Whoopie Pies

Whoopie pies are the official Maine snack. The world's largest whoopie pie was made in South Portland on March 26, 2011. It weighed 1,062 pounds, and pieces of it were sold to fund sending whoopie pies to soldiers overseas. (a Bath café)

Clams

Soft-shell steamer clams burrow in the sand and are harvested year-round with a clam hoe. These clams are the most commonly harvested in Maine. (Sagadahoc Bay, Georgetown)

Blueberries

Maine leads the world in the production of wild blueberries. They were named the official state berry in 1991, and blueberry pie was named the official Maine dessert.

Blueberries were originally harvested by hand with a rake that was invented in Maine. Today they are harvested with machines, unless the terrain is too rocky. Blueberries are harvested from late July to early September. (Ellsworth)

Chickadees

The black-capped chickadee was named the Maine state bird in 1927. The chickadee lives year-round in Maine. It eats seeds, berries, and bugs and hides its food in the crevices of tree bark. It returns later to eat what it has hidden. The chickadee mates for life, and both parents take care of their young. (Library Park Gazebo, Bath)

WENDY ULMER is a former music and English teacher with a Master of Education in the Creative Arts in Learning from Lesley University, Boston. *My Twelve Maine Christmas Days* is her fourth children's book. Her first book, *A Campfire for Cowboy Billy*, is a Taylor Trade paperback. *A Isn't for Fox* and *Zero, Zilch, Nada: Counting to None* were both published with Sleeping Bear Press. Wendy lives in Arrowsic, Maine.

SANDY CRABTREE graduated from Arcadia University in Pennsylvania with a BFA in painting. Sandy is a strong advocate for the visual arts. She has taught for more than forty years, and her artwork is in many private and corporate collections. Through her artwork, Sandy strives to inspire a sense of responsibility to preserve the enormous beauty of the natural world, and to cherish the peace and solitude it provides. She lives in Bath, Maine, with her husband, Richard.

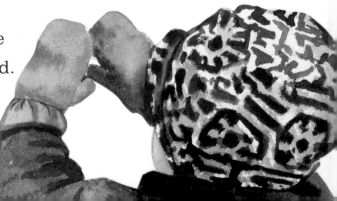